THAT ROCKS!

SEDIMENTARY ROCKS

By Maria Nelson

Gareth Stevens
Publishing

Please visit our website, www.garethstevens.com. For a free color catalog of all our high-quality books, call toll free 1-800-542-2595 or fax 1-877-542-2596.

Library of Congress Cataloging-in-Publication Data

Library of Congress Cataloging-in-Publication Data

Nelson, Maria.
Sedimentary rocks / Maria Nelson.
    p. cm. — (That rocks!)
Includes index.
ISBN 978-1-4339-8322-1 (pbk.)
ISBN 978-1-4339-8323-8 (6-pack)
ISBN 978-1-4339-8321-4 (library binding)
1. Sedimentary rocks—Juvenile literature. I. Title.
QE471.N47 2014
552'.5—dc23
                                2012047237

First Edition

Published in 2014 by
Gareth Stevens Publishing
111 East 14th Street, Suite 349
New York, NY 10003

Copyright © 2014 Gareth Stevens Publishing

Designer: Katelyn Londino
Editor: Kristen Rajczak

Photo credits: Cover, p. 1 PRILL Mediendesign und Fotografie/Shutterstock.com; p. 5 Dudarev Mikhail/Shutterstock.com; p. 7 repox/Shutterstock.com; p. 9 marmo81/Shutterstock.com; p. 11 © iStockphoto.com/kojihirano; p. 12 (inset) commons.wikimedia.org/wiki/File:Lehigh_conglom.jpg/Wikipedia.org; p. 13 BIOPHOTO ASSOCIATES/Photo Researchers/Getty Images; p. 15 Christopher Elwell/Shutterstock.com; p. 17 Oliver Strewe/Lonely Planet Images/Getty Images; p. 19 Don W Fawcett/Photo Researchers/Getty Images; p. 20 (inset) © iStockphoto.com/travelpixpro.

Printed in the United States of America

CPSIA compliance information: Batch #CS13GS: For further information contact Gareth Stevens, New York, New York at 1-800-542-2595.

CONTENTS

Words in the glossary appear in **bold** type the first time they are used in the text.

WHAT ARE SEDIMENTARY ROCKS?

Most of Earth is made of metamorphic and igneous rock. These rocks commonly form under hot conditions, often under Earth's surface. The rock we're most familiar with is sedimentary rock. It makes up less than 1 percent of Earth's **volume**, but 75 percent of its land surface!

From the sandy shores of Florida's beaches to the limestone of the Great Pyramid in Egypt, sedimentary rocks can be found all over the world. These rocks are made up of **sediment** that has been **compacted**.

SET IN STONE

Sedimentary petrology (puh-TRAH-luh-jee) is the study of the occurrence and makeup of sedimentary rocks.

The Great Pyramid in Egypt is built from blocks of limestone, a sedimentary rock.

CREATING SEDIMENT

Sediment is created by weathering. Weathering is the breakdown of rock by wind and water. Sand, soil, and clay are all examples of sediment that **physical** weathering can create.

Chemical weathering also creates sediment. New matter, such as water, may be introduced to rock and cause it to soften or break down. Then, it becomes easier for physical weathering to occur. The introduction of gases, such as oxygen or carbon dioxide, to a rock also commonly causes chemical weathering.

SET IN STONE

The process of water combining with matter in a rock and causing it to break down is called hydrolysis.

Sediment is often found at the bottom of lakes and rivers—or where lakes and rivers used to be!

7

MOVING ON

Sedimentary rock formation begins when sediment is blown away by wind, carried by water currents, or pulled by **gravity** down a hill or mountain. The movement of sediment away from its starting place is called erosion.

Sediment contains many tiny pieces of rock. As wind and water carry them, they bump and slide against each other. This makes them smooth and round, and may sort them by size or type of rock. After a time, sediment settles in a new place.

SET IN STONE

Sediment settles where it does because the energy of the wind or water carrying it becomes too weak to keep moving the sediment.

Weathering can create sediment from any existing rock.

ROCK SOLID

Once sediment settles, other matter builds up on top of it and presses on it. Animals and humans may walk on it. Water can flow over it. Over time, the sediment is buried. The tiny pieces that make up the sediment are compacted as the **pressure** on the sediment increases.

Water mixed with **minerals** may flow into the sediment, filling open spaces in the forming rock. This helps bind the rock together. The rock will continue to be compacted as it's buried deeper—perhaps by more sediment settling above it!

SET IN STONE

The changes a sedimentary rock undergoes while buried—from compaction brought on by increased pressure to the introduction of water mixtures—is called diagenesis (dy-uh-JEH-nuh-suhs).

The scientific term for sediment being compacted and bound together to form rock is "lithification" (lih-thuh-fuh-KAY-shun).

CLASTIC SEDIMENTARY ROCK

There are two main kinds of sedimentary rocks. The first, called clastic sedimentary rock, forms from sediment created by the weathering explained earlier in this book. It's the most common kind of sedimentary rock and is often made up of minerals found on Earth's surface, such as quartz.

Clastic sedimentary rock may also have pieces of shells, pebbles, and other objects compacted in it. All the bits—big or small—that make up clastic sedimentary rock are called clasts.

conglomerate

SET IN STONE

Conglomerate is one kind of sedimentary rock that has rounded clasts in it that are more than 0.08 inch (2 mm) around.

Breccia (BREH-chee-uh) also has easily seen clasts in it, but they're jagged and uneven looking.

ORGANIC SEDIMENTARY ROCK

The second grouping of sedimentary rocks is nonclastic sedimentary rock. Scientists call one type organic sedimentary rocks since they're made of the remains of living things. Some organic sedimentary rocks come from the shells of tiny sea creatures, such as plankton. Others come from the sediment created by dead plant matter.

While their sediment is different from that of clastic sedimentary rocks, the lithification of nonclastic sedimentary rock is the same. Sediment settles and, over time, is buried under pressure.

SET IN STONE

Sedimentary rock sometimes forms because of chemical processes in the ocean. Minerals build up in areas that start to dry out and become nonclastic sedimentary rock.

The sedimentary rock halite may form chemically in the ocean. You might know halite by another name—rock salt!

FOSSIL FUELS

Sedimentary rocks are very important to people. Their formation has produced important natural resources—fossil fuels. Fossil fuels come from the remains of long dead plants and animals, and can be used to make energy.

One kind of fossil fuel that lithification creates is coal. Organic sedimentary rock that forms from compacted plant matter becomes peat. Then, over time and with increased temperature and pressure, peat becomes coal. Both coal and peat can be used to make power and heat.

SET IN STONE

Fossil fuels are a limited resource that can't be found everywhere. Much of the world's oil comes from sedimentary rock found in Middle Eastern countries.

This pile of peat will be used for fuel.

STRATIFICATION

Many sedimentary rocks have strata, or layers. They're on top of one another and look like stripes! The strata can be different colors and thicknesses, depending on where the rock's sediment came from, how much settled there, and its mineral makeup.

The formation of strata is called bedding or stratification (stra-tuh-fuh-KAY-shun). One kind of stratification is graded bedding, in which clasts are sorted by size. The largest pebbles commonly settle on the bottom, and the fine grains on top. Their order can be opposite, too!

SET IN STONE

Strata near the bottom of a sedimentary rock are older than those near the top.

Sedimentary rock strata can be cross-bedded, like the rock shown here. The strata are slanted in the direction that wind or water was moving when the sediment settled.

LAYERS OF HISTORY

Sedimentary rocks tell us a lot about Earth's history. They may contain fossils, which are the remains or marks of past plants and animals. Scientists use fossils to find out what life was like in an area thousands—or even millions—of years ago!

Scientists study the order of sedimentary rock strata, size and shape of clasts, and rocks' mineral makeup, too. These can show whether sediment was moved by wind, water, or gravity—and even how fast those forces moved it!

Fossils found in sedimentary rocks help scientists understand how landforms and weather have changed over time.

HOW DO CLASTIC SEDIMENTARY ROCKS FORM?

weathering breaks down existing rock, creating sediment

wind, water, and gravity move sediment

sediment settles

sediment is buried

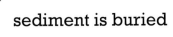

water and mineral mixtures help bind sediment together into rock

pressure increases and sediment is compacted

GLOSSARY

chemical: having to do with matter that can be mixed with other matter to cause changes

compact: to force closer together

gravity: the force that pulls objects toward Earth's center

mineral: matter in the ground that forms rocks

physical: having to do with natural science

pressure: the application of force

sediment: matter, such as stones and sand, that is carried onto land or into the water by wind, water, or land movement

volume: the amount of space an object takes up

FOR MORE INFORMATION

Books

Bryan, Bethany. *How the Rock Cycle Works.* New York, NY: PowerKids Press, 2009.

Hyde, Natalie. *What Are Sedimentary Rocks?* New York, NY: Crabtree Publishing, 2011.

Websites

Cycles: The Rock Cycle
www.cotf.edu/ete/modules/msese/earthsysflr/rock.html
Read about how rocks form and see an illustration of the rock cycle.

Sedimentary Rocks
geology.com/rocks/sedimentary-rocks.shtml
Look through a picture gallery of many kinds of sedimentary rocks.

INDEX